LYRICAL MUSINGS

by

SOUMEN ROY

COVER & INTERIOR DESIGN BY
LITEROMA

Lyrical Musings

Powered By

Literoma Inc.

Your one stop solution for Author Branding, Book Publishing Services, Creative Excellence, Book & Art Promotions.

604, Loharuka Greens,
VIP Road, KaziNazrul Islam Avenue
Kolkata – 700052

Email:*literoma.publishingservices@gmail.com*

Blog:*literomagroup.blogspot.com*

Facebook: *www.facebook.com/literomagroup*

Book Store:*https://literoma.stores.instamojo.com/*

Ph: +91 93309 19306

Disclaimer

ABOUT BOOK

Poetry is a song of hearts that celebrates life with love in every corner of earth with grace and gratitude, since love is the only one thing that turns the world go around. Lyrical Musings celebrates life in its own spice of varieties and experiences. Sometimes in little things, nature, spirituality, emotions dark and grey blossoming in beauty, of the ordeals around us within and society.

ABOUT AUTHOR

Soumen Roy is a professional writer and a triple lingual poet. Apart from poetry, he writes quotes, stories and articles. His debut novel Scar has been published recently. His writing is unique and contains depth. His works have been published in more than 30 anthologies, magazines and newspapers. He's been launched on an international platform in a book Chimes and Rhymes by renowned Dawn Marie publication, then in Carlos Luis Betrayal and later on, he's been co-author under reputed publications like Viswabharti, SathiyaAnand etc. His poetry has been a part of the international poetry festival in Guntur; he is also a part of Langlit and Literarycognizanc, an international peer-reviewed Journal and so on. He likes photography and painting and is also fond of music. Currently, his Bangla poetry book Ontoral is under publication.

POEM: 1
Waiting For The Spring

Waiting for the
spring
My heart started
singing
Drenched in the droplets
of love
My eyes sparkled with joy, and
happiness was gleaming.

The universe seemed to be
so friendly
Lurches into my heart,
juggling
Exploring the numerous
doors of cheer
I moved ahead with all my faith,
Oh, dear.

Raining droplets of spring soothe my heart with
blessings s
I moved ahead with all my faith in loving. With a heart
filled with gratitude and forgiveness, I smiled
In the spring, for that, I have been kept waiting.

POEM: 2
Ode to Poetry

Poetry is there where there is peace
Expressive and alluring over the ivory sheets
Where there is no more fatigue
Poetry is the melodious song of hearts full of life.

Poetry is the mirror which turns distorted things into
beauty
Poetry smiles with hope, a prayer offered to the almighty
Poetry is the kindle into the darkness of nights
Poetry is the firefly that adds meaning to life.

Poetry travels to the deepest of inner consciousness
Poetry is the canvas painting life always with happiness
Poetry travels all around nature, connecting every
emotion
Where dreams come true, gleaming with love and
forgiveness.

POEM: 3
Heavenly Guitar

Song of every heart in the strings of the guitar
Enchanting melodies resonate in the air
Love-laden notes with a smile and cares
Love is raining with joy and singing in the air.

Love is the most wonderful feeling that can be found
everywhere
Magical drops of due with affection and care
Love is a nourishing smile and a beautiful prayer
Holding lots of grace and gratitude, love is a song of a
heavenly guitar.

Love is everywhere, in the rays of sunshine
In the lullabies of air
In the tweeter of chirping birds
Love is the beautiful flower with the sweetest nectar.

Love is within us, and we are made to love each other
For love has no reason just to be happy with one another
Love has been mercy, rests on every one of us
Love is God, a unified religion connecting with faith in
the entire universe!

POEM: 4
Yearning

Heart with
yearning
Glittering eyes with lots
of hopes yawning
Recalling the memories
left in bygones
Will one come to fetch him in between wrecked lanes
full of venoms?
Never lose hope, will chase the destiny
Since he is a child of light and a saga of longing
symphony.
Lost in between faces
He is now a sufferer
of calamity
Yet his eyes refuse to lose
a bit of shine
Without a roof and repose, he dwells
in between unknown identities.
Every morning he runs to lift
heavy gunny bags
Cleaning the train compartments and picking up plastic
bottles out of rags
With lots of yearning
within his heart
He slept in a railway
compartment, so very tired.
Wheel of Fortune was
rolling on his side
Blew the whistle, and the train
left with the boy sleeping inside
Who knows the plan of
destiny?
Destiny runs with its own plans

and scrutiny
Wakes up the child in between
unfamiliar crowd
Someone patted his shoulder, standing behind him with
a voice polite and loud
In utter vexation, he discovered
the hope in the joy
Saw his teacher filled with teary eyes, a melting allow.
Brimming with joy, a gleam
upon his face
Reached out to his parents with
delight and grace
Since he never learned to give up
in the race of life
Being honest in every action, he thanked God for paving
his way with mercy and grace in his strife.

POEM: 5
Ode to Republic Day

Celebrating Republic Day Standing
on the most pious soil
Tricolour waving uncoil
The struggle for glory and the song of
pride
Saga of sacrifices with courage
dynamite
They went laughing and singing
on the noose
Faced the cruel gunshots made by the
invaders without any excuse
They stood against the grand cannons, which blew them
into pieces
Imagine just how brave they were and
their sacrifices
Their blood boiled to see their country's
freedom in shackles
They felt so blessed with the rigorous oath they had
taken against every oppression
They lived and died protecting the glory of soil
In the wake of dawn, they defeated the
invaders,
gaining victory over turmoils
Freedom was never so easy neither the flag blows
because of the wind
It only happened of the dare of the Bravehearts and their
dedicated patriotic incline
They are yet engaged in frightful
missions
Chilling nights full of snow, they are singing for the
nation
With unconditional love, they are our closest friend

Brave of bravest with the chest of iron stakes their well-
being and keep going us defend
Each and every second, they ensure our
safety
They die our deaths in the cruel hands
of enemy
My heart cries in pain, waving storms insane in my lane
They are not only our saviour but our living God,
protecting us from enemies' brutal cane
What we have done for them, just
a candle in their name!

O', "Come on", just to blame the politicians isn't a matter
of shame
Guns and cannons, here and there, singing and saluting
their grand courage
I do also salute every single brave heart and pay my
homage
Shall I bring home some soil from the borders of the
country where they stand as an undefeatable wall
Worshipping those boots of strength, I wish to shun my
weakness and stand like a tree tall
Endless glory wrapped in valour
Merciless bombing runs ahead. My soldier
Just a thought gives me goosebumps, and I pray for their
safety
Fortunate are those parents who nurture them with
discipline, sacrifice and bravery
I feel so proud of my brothers and sisters serving the
country
Come, let's sing the national anthem in honour of them
and their country's mother's dignity.

POEM: 6
Shiva – The Divine Beauty

Shiva is beauty
Beauty is Shiva
Everything that is beautiful lies in Shiva
In the glory of sunshine, in between the blossoming
flowers
also, he smiles in the giggle of a flowing river
The tranquil divine truth lies everywhere
In the purity of devotions, in the innocence of a smile
in every jingle of nature
The kind austere sitting over Nandi, with a trident in
hand and everything
lies in his Trinetra.
The Adi Yoga is the divine shine of truth
The ultimate source of happiness and wisdom
Beyond birth and death, Shiva lies in conscious freedom
The holy Belpatra smells of heaven of love
Shrine of peace flapping in the wings of a dove!

POEM: 7
Best Love Story

God might be busy writing the best love story
For them, love seemed to be life, and life seemed such a
beauty
Smile sailed in the corners of the lips for no reason
Each and every moment seemed to be just happy.
As if someone playing violin and guitar
That very moment love stepped into their life and was all
over the air
Books remained closed, and they refused to study
Love was sonorous, playing the sweetest melody
They were made for each other, and love was made for
thee
Remained unspoken but said everything silently
They were made to love each other, not to be with one
another
Love was painful that they borrowed forever
Love is not the name of getting peace every time
but love was a complete surrender
They lived with love being parted forever.

POEM: 8
Blissful Love

God might be busy writing the
best love story
Krishna played the magical flute
for his beloved Radharani
Love is life, and so life turned
into beauty
Radharani smiled, pouring bliss into Krishna's melody
A love that was so pure and kept
resonating heavenly
Two bodies, one soul breathing on
each other,
Ah! What divine glory!
Painted the sky full of blue, held the flowers for the sake
of love
Love is devotion and mercy
into the wings of a dove
They lived in love forever, being
parted together
For love is not only the name of getting,
its peace in complete surrender.

POEM: 9
Canvas of Poet

Infinite mind
Infinite thoughts
Spiders web
Mirror concave
Spirits of a flying bird in the smile of ink
Weaving imagination blotting over heartbeats
Romantic dilute in the lands silvery
Sublime serenity in the canvas of hearts
The pensive aroma in the lonesome desert
Oasis quenching the thirst of the weary travellers
Infinite messages decor in a poet's canvas
Hues of love smiling in glee
Song of calmness flowing in the sea
Song of nature rejuvenating creation
Words of pearl connecting every heart and emotion
Infinite mind, infinite thoughts
Gardening life in a poet's canthus.

POEM: 10
Complete Painting

Hues of red, blue and crimson
She is a tale of colourful shades, a sublime orientation
Stepped ahead, she is a perfect balance of grey, purple and green
She paints herself in the glory of roses with a saffron attire,
for the sufferings
She swings with her colours, Autumn and Spring
Hugs all the colours of life, a blissful smiling canvas
She is a portrait of life, a complete painting.

POEM: 11
Ode To My Brother

Showers of rain falling all over
With joy
Lurches the glorious convoy
Masculine shoulders love laden
Matches ahead my selfless
Warrior
O', he looks so very humble.

Tears roll down my cheeks, and my breath remains
beholden
I grew up in those hands of care
In thy shelter, a protective mountain.
Feeling sort of words today in the sheets of expression
A monk of tranquillity smiles in my heart, diving into
thou ocean.
So vast beyond the vastness of seas and ocean
There lies so much for one and all
Conquer of hearts and lives; he seems a tale of
benevolence
Standing as a tree tall.
Thou work, worship, and justice always remains at their
peak
Words and principles matter only,
Never controls anybody
Beyond the narrow meanders flowing the unbiased sea
Living life in service and sacrifices,
My loving brother is he.

POEM: 12
Holi - The Basantutsab

Rejoicing the festival of the spring
saying," Happy Holi."
First greetings to the Lord,
to friends and family.

Preaching the colours of harmony
Holi shatters among many
Celebrating love and brotherhood
Holi spreads the colours of gratitude.

I wish you all " play Holi."
with colours and gulal,
Can't resist my excitement
It's Holi, after all.

The festival of colours is
Bringing immeasurable joy
Each face is smiling
To celebrate and enjoy.

I wish to paint myself within my heart
Even in the yards with multiple colours.

I wish to play with my friends, to colour their faces
Throwing buckets of coloured water
bringing the grace.

I don't even hesitate to wet the girls
A scope to get close with multiple colours.

I wish to burn the Holikawith joy and happiness,
Signifying the evil overpowered with devotion and
merriness.

Holi memorialises the Raas Lila
the love tale of Radha Krishna
Traditional Holi brings more grace
to colour the Lord's feet at temple gates.

I wish to have the bhang laddus
and dance with drums
I wish to sign "Holi Hai" and make some noise with fun.

I wish to visit every door with gulal in my hands,
To decorate the elderly feet and colour the young.
I wish to have lovely sweets,
a special treat from everyone.

Every corner seems to be a rainbow
with colours and gulal, Saying "Holi Hai."
I wish to return with limpid aglow.

But I still miss the colours on my face
decored with love
I rejoice in my rich cultural heritage.
Wishing a Happy Holi to all.

POEM: 13
The Canvas Of Life

My life, an azure new canvas,
in the form of art
by the humble touch of a brush
A colourful journey to start.

Sketched by trembling hands
portrays my life on the colourful canvas
That reflects my confessions;
spreading among colourful dimensions.

The panorama of life has been sketched enormously
To know the unknown ones,
the paintbrush is being splashed rigorously.
Discovering my true colour
and spreading it everywhere
I paint my life with originality,
with the gentle touch of reality.

I do paint myself in childhood,
sweet and gracious,
full of naughty innocence.
Discovering the Pastel Pinks;
always stands for innocence that winks.

Painting myself with the super soul
For full of love for the clutching babies
and compassion for the old.
To discover the colourful Blue;
That always stands for divine love is absolutely true.
 I do paint myself as a truant boy who makes jokes,
and create laughter to conquest the Yellow colour;
for the laughter to recur ever after.

I do paint myself as a teenager;
Searching for intimate love and passion
To explore the Red colour;
deluged in loveable passion,
in the eyes of creation.

I do paint myself as a young man
Who never fails the strength to conquer,
I wish to discover the Green colour
That stands to symbolise strength as the conquering of
fear.

I do paint myself in my victory;
which brings many successful glories
To find the Golden colour
for I could celebrate a successful journey.

I do paint myself in my effort;
to achieve my desired resort,
to discover the Silver colour;
anticipating my efforts.

I wish I could recreate myself as a scholar;
which brings some pride mingled in an endeavour,
Discovering the Purple colour;
for everyone's proud elevator.

I do paint myself as an achiever;
full with wealth and desire
Discovering the Orange colour;
to rejoice in my wealth and desire.

I do paint myself as an old man
full with dejection
To discover the grey colour;
to participate in my dejected metaphor!

POEM: 14
Life's Adjustment

The purpose of life lies in
Positivity,
To accept the odds and
ends in reality.

The substance of life showed
by our forefathers,
New cultivation after
every disaster.

Learn from the mistakes
of life,
Some to reject,
Some accept,
Follow the wise.

You are not a fool,
Be strong and cool,
Don't be confused!

Leave your childishness,
Mature yourself to avoid
the mess.

Why wear that shoe,
That doesn't suit you?
If the shoe is suppressed
and don't fit; then
Leave it
but
treasure it as a lesson
for you will have to get skilful creation!

You are polished enough,
To avoid the toilsome
snuff,
Why do you fear?
o 'my dear!

Don't force to adjust in
such a shoe,
It's not made for you,
don't waste a single tear
a moment,
Don't allow it to be recurrent.

Ever after,
That's why you,
How could you adjust
that shoe!!
You are not dull,
stand like a tree tall,
Though clever enough.

Silence speaks your's
Intelligence,
It will bring the crusade
without any violence,
Even Einstein was in fear,
Just remember,
Oh, dear.

NEWTON EXCELLENT MIND,
Gallileo, Extraordinary mind,
Soumen, please, never mind!!!!!!!!

When he was in standard
Two,
Can't utter a single word,

But today, the world salute
that master,
same with Sir Newton.....

Oh, My dear!
In order to carry your
positive action,
you must
develop a positive vision.

Forget all past happenings
in your shoe of
self-confidence,
No one will help you.

Be a follower of those wise,
Do realise,
You have to perform with
self-actions For Him.

Peaceful co-existence lies
in patience,
Nothing is uncomfortable
in the realistic decision.
Don't forget!

History will remember
you for your courage
and celestial vision.

POEM: 15

Rain

Monsoon alarmingly came again,
With abundant showers of rain,
Pouring heavily salty pangs in the
memories lane.

Melancholic tears to weep
lots of pain,
While I am searching for my beloved brother, who was
lost in the drained ashes with rain,
Eyes getting filled with tears again
I can't remind when the brutal thunder had cared for my
loss or gain.

My heart is pounding, writhing in
Nostalgia,
Never had I thought I had to decor his
pyre with fire,
Rain will never quench the heat of
my burning eyes,
Cruel thunder has come again to repeat those memories
with brother, in disguise.

Vacant eyes still haunt every
alleys,
From childhood to hospital,
hospital to home everywhere
with negative replies,
The drizzles were joyful sometimes,
with paper boats.

Playing in the spalshing pools of water together,
our joy floats,
Who knows its cruelty in the attire of

Flood,
Doctors gave a death certificate,
My brother in blood.

My brother used to carry me to school,
Left me mourning,
Sorrows of salty water are to have remained
Within countless rain.

POEM: 16
If

If life is not within a soft and hard coconut
Oasis seems thirsty in an arid desert
Unspoken delivered ignorance
Perceiving corpse reticence

If life is not a tale of dusk and dawn
Shades of diverse colours can't be portrayed
in thy lawn
Swinging between giggles and yawn
Guffaws of Sore and merry cuddles, a venerable song

If life is not a tale of love
Compassion won't be a soothing bud
Life is a tale of romance
Sweetest desert of hearts, a fragrant aroma of eloquent
fragrance

If life is not a crafted theatre
Lessons can't flourish in their meanders
Stumbles a must obligatory
Ultimate surrender to the omnipotent visionary.

POEM: 17
Kalsi

Sipping the divine nectar
of creativity,
Smile devoted to the creative
Austerity.
Glows faith, full of devotion,
Pouring the cool, silent ocean.
Descends the bliss, softening the
rigid roots,
Grasping the placid
Pursuits.
Smile the faithful in
Devotion,
In between creatures and endless
Creation.
Chirping birds tweeting
Rhymes,
Embraces the aura of cuddling
Chimes.
Song of Eve comes in
Prayers,
Blew the conch shell, a devoted
Surrender.
The merciful veil in tomorrow's waist,
Celestial glow pours in haste.

POEM: 18
Bonding With The Nature

Descends paradise on earth bonding
with nature,
The glee of mirth engulfs a
sublime attire.
Green, full of green with a beam
of life-bearing harmonical signature,
Hail thou spring with colourful
Luster.
Breeze shatters merriness, a zeal
as metaphor,
Blossoming fragrant flowers
enhalos a devotional nectar.
Butterflies dance in the
palanquin of spring,
Colouring hearts so expressive, vivid
and refreshing.

POEM: 19
The Song Of Nature

Bountiful of love, all
around me,
The song of nature
seems like motherly.

The golden rays from
heaven
Rejuvenates creation,
Travelling from mountains
reaches the land and
oceans.

The affectionate tale of
determination,
The song of
nature,
Excess of love, all
around me,
The song is about nature
seems so motherly.

The golden rays from
Heaven,
Beautifies the creation,
Travelling from mountains
reaches the land and
oceans.

The affectionate tale of
Love and creation,
Radiating lively hopes to
flourish as a fountain,
A humble touch of

concern
with caring attention,
The lovely feeling
with gentle emotion.

Dancing harmony in
the lap of green,
The sun-kissed daffodils
rests
in the palanquin of spring,
The ever-flowing
of dreamy breeze,
smiles between the
Lovely new leaves.

Tranquillity flows as
drizzles over a river,
care recurs with her exotic
smell
providing the warmth of
mother.

The pleasing nights
encourages with lullabies
chasing the
merriness, with
positive advice.
Radiating lively hopes to
flourish as a fountain,
A humble touch of concern
with caring attention.

The lovely feeling
with gentle emotion,
Dancing harmony in
the lap of green.

The wrinkled tried rests
in the palanquin of spring,
The never-ending flow
of shooting breeze,
Smiles between the
Lovely new leaves.

Tranquillity flows as
drizzles over the river,
care recurs with her exotic
smell
providing the warmth of the mother.

The pleasing nights
encourages
with lullabies
chasing the
merriness, with
positive advice.

POEM: 20
My Beloved Maa

Maa is the first word spoken.
The divine creation
The tale of love and emotion
The never-ending flow of caring notion
She is the deity of kindness and compassion
Her smile is the ultimate comfort and consolation
Her presence brings a feeling of secureness and strength
in the realisation.
Her lap is my safest place, with lots of affection
She is lovely with her kisses, hugs and smile of
attraction
She brings courage with lots of inspiration
She is a glorious composition
Far beyond imagination
The caring institution
Without any sort of expectations.
She is my mirror reflection,
detects me by reading my face
She is my encouragement,
to stand up after every failure in life's race
She is my heaven,
supports me in everything with positive vibes
She is my pride
guides me to follow the honest track of life
She is the motivation,
Who disciplined and bolstered my dreams
She is next to God,
my creator protecting me from all sorts of screams
She is my friend more than a teacher
She is my lovely Maa, my moral guide and philosopher.
Every morning before I rise,
I find her near to me so early

Every night when she goes to sleep,
she kisses my forehead with lots of blessings
When she is not at home, I feel very lonely
But I find my peace by smelling her saree
I always wish to rest on her lap
in her charming lullabies
Every day we kiss each other,
seems so very lovely.

Maa, you are the only one.
My love, devotion, smile and fun
You are my heart and soul
Without you, I am an empty bowl.

POEM: 21
Heaven On Earth

The aves in the snow
Twittering in the trees
Swings of heavenly breeze
Spick hedonic waves of utopia
Muster of glee,
dilutes heaven on earth
Reaping chic canorous leash
Canopus yoke mesmerising galloping
delightful frenzy
Fairies descend with clusters of pearls,
searing orientation restoring grace
Glittering in the wings, flapping emblaze
Melodies reverie in warble,
jovial in the shiny snowy spread
Aves trills merry in the conscious vale.

POEM: 22
Solitary

The flow is uneven,
A song without lyrics,
Cellar of unenlightenment
Remorseless in solitary confinement.

Sunbathing in the sand on the solitary shore
Gleams upon faces seducing galore.
Pride and prejudices thrashing coastal sides
Tear, thus, speaks brightly.

The bird flies high, leaving the cage of solitudes
Gaining wisdom to the wings of flight,
Solitudeness sings its solitary heights
A due upon hearts, envisioning proper delights.

POEM: 23
Hymns

Tired with life
Suffocating solace
O thou loving vase
Will you call my days
The ashes won't howl lacking; it's grey
Succumbed weariness bulldozing my heart
Crafted hymns shedding tears
Waterfalls short of softening the heart
Can't hear the noise of the temple
Divine soothes me in oneness
Sometimes or you
Life's sickle to the lands of rescue
Salted due.

POEM: 24
Touch

Soft tenderness smiling blooms with innocence,
Overruns glee in chocolate of brilliance
"Touch" tell-tale a mischief impudence,
Harmless hugs envisages a malice auction of emotions
Gigglings weep in bitter silence
Unaware touch in a playful emergence
Scar of scratches
countless wound touches
Panicking tears,
Stainless heart trapped in cozen bane.
Blood-curling eyes frozen
Refuse the touch; insane
"Oh! Can you hear my pain,
I do promise I will never ask for any more chocolates
again."

POEM: 25
Cherish

I wish I could cry,
And cry to settle my pain
To pull off all those curtains of Illusions
Dancing merrily at the window,
Never meant for my glow.
I don't wish to act more and more,
Wish to float and lay beside the shore
The story no more.
Wishes left me many years ago,
Tears of stone are not meant to flow.
Salts of destiny
Draws a line sailing its agony.
Don't want any water to quench my thirst
I am a cactus thorn to bleed in the crucified desert
Waiting long, I owe to the vulture
To Offer my flesh yet a corpus, complete to the creature.
Wishes are no more to wish
Don't want a moment turning back to cherish,
I have smiled long in the attire of greyish
Cheated myself. I am a dull story fading so lavish.
Curtains are heavy and can't flow in pain
Dry leaves of tomorrow ruling in the lane
Yet more between present sorrow
Crossing the bar just remained a wish
Succumbed between breathing, I
am a ceasing wish
Don't know the meaning of wish
Cheated myself with the word named cherish!

POEM: 26
Residual

When I will die
The body will remain astray
The residual left in ashes will lack all its grey
All lust and pride will fade away
Don't even know if my body will receive a wreath or
wry.

My existence will be the residual between you; perhaps
you will recall my memories someday,

Please, my dear and near ones,
don't bring a single tear
My soul will rest in peace if you mourn my demise.

I will be a lost entity in the pages of history
I will embark on a new journey with a completely new
story
My eyes will get a new vision of the chapter on a blind
person
Nourishing and chasing those incomplete dreams with
proper curious action.

Hope my death will be a perfect smile, even up to a
single
Hope my residual will not go in vain but rather be a
cause enough to some specific jingle

The motto of life is to live to its fullest
Residual of life is not limited to the four shoulders of
fittest
Before saying goodbye, it's better to be modest!

POEM: 27
Alone

The crowds left me alone.
Throwing stones repeatedly
Blood curling eyes thudding, alights a sudden
thunderbolt
Autistic child breathing life's zeal and poison
Revolting questions, why not me?
Inseparable in thy lotus feet
Unuttered few forsaken the boon of beauty to be in ashes
The bipolar mind of mine swinging all around, leaving
thou poison alone
Embolden my spirit in rustic attire,
Stabbing the dampened lustre
Leaving the crowd alone
Bygone be bygones.

POEM: 28
Passion

My passion is natures child reaping crops of love
Pollinating a lyrical flow, soothing solitude in weary
summer
The glee of breeze loving thou heart, reaping crops of
faith
Beyond horizon inseminating new hopes full of mirth
A divine trinity of imagination, trust and oneness
Passion in the attire of flora and fauna goes green and
green
Vivid, expressive and alive
Overflows compassion from the mountain vale
Spa, refreshing soul
Peeps the moon with a humble kiss of affection,
in the palanquin of lullabies
Passion runs all over nature,
in each and every corner
Smiling between heart, creativity and creature
Glisten admits as a twinkling star.

POEM: 29
Romantic Ballad

Perspiration of your warmth and heat
Striking the belly, midnight
Soft tendrils wrapping my whole
Kisses so lofty
Enraging the embraces
Clusters of clutches
Hooks of scarlet enjoys without bracelet
Over your breast, my passion arouses a founding
sensation
Close proximity with comfortable release
A tight and silky tender touch,
clings hours together
Hugs of fire breathing over my chest
Innocence peeps within, blooming aroma
Fragrant rose in silvery moonlit
Revealing secrets with an enthusiastic gaze
She smiles; the night turns a tale
Sweetest gale, a sagacious sale!

POEM: 30
Reticent Passion

Blithe song of rain
Pouring love from heaven
Phantom of delight
Gleams upon sight
Passionate unfolded composition
of lips in the rain
Sensuous glee enters my heart's secret chamber
A lovely silent auction of emotions flutters
Half smile beckons a lyrical invitation
Irresistible sensuous art
Outpouring virgin desert
Angelic beauty simmering in impulsive warm,
breathable fluttering emotional joyous.
Fluttering desire records lovely sunrise
as plumes over sunflower
Heat in the rain beholden love paradise to
suck thy nectar
Gestures of myriad tranquil feelings in thy
turquoise eyes.
Sailing romance in thou embrace with
insane heartbeats.

POEM: 31
Naked Swords

Naked swords
needling over ivory sheets
Kindling the abysmal ravine
Bleeding silence, a wallow-in a grin
Beyond the dongs of rusted charms
Guffaws the glitter of a stagnant pendulum
A tale of lost aristocracy in aristocratic wines
Screams the woman in disgust
Streaking pully with blisters on her palms
Suffers her anchal of clemency
Consoling with a drip of water to the parched lips
Raising high from the darts of blood
Warrior of warriors galloping in the crescent moon
Wandering in cool
The aroma of coffee synthesising the nerves
Removing the stains, rumbling rummage with pen and
paper
In the flight of angelic storm.

POEM: 32
Conflict

Jotted clots of bipolarity create unrest in the mind
Disgraceful corruption corrupts man's mind
Confused sage in the trap of volcanic eruption
Molecules of liberalisation engrossed in chaos and confusion
Sage eyes wear the lens, assuming and dull
Dwelling with the conflicts, unhygienic within the skull
Aeons of storms gush with thunderbolts
Monks of peace trapped within greyish revolts
Drizzles on thy temple pour its ceasefire
Scars of illiteracy howling, a dark vampire
Anatomy of enlightenment in the library of conscience
Satisfaction of souls wrapped within self possessions
Revealing the chapters' full content
Hallucinations of disagreements, a stressful discernment
Commitment to harmony, a squirrel glee
Monks of monastery forgiving disagree
Debris of conflict in the hive of bee
Sipping the divine, smile sails its tranquillity in its biographical sea!

POEM: 33
Ode To Father

Sun of thunder
inside the womb of clouds-
Smiles with firmness with
Raining mould.
Each drop moulds
billions courage
Cultivating inspiration, removing
damages.
Ploughing fertility inseminating
seeds of hope
Fertilising sage with a cane
of effort,
Pollinating yards of barren to
enfold,
Waves of green in governed
zygote
Voracious ploughs with a dearth of
segmentation,
Crops of sudorreporinfruitation
Son of thunder born to face
thou simmer.
Songs of ash for a mortal glimmer
Bleeding irrigation landscaping sunny
core
Monitoring thou zeal to cultivate joy.

POEM: 34
Gleam

Wrinkles over lustre
Teens with green liquor
Sways thy memories
Hiss of spring vagaries
Rhymes of hangover
Waltz of spring choir
Rejecting the rotten skin
Spark of sun gleaming
Resetting tidal efflux
Undying perennial bask.

POEM: 35
Lore

Glamorous peaks smile with lofty cara
Cottage with bullock buddies, a green aura
Vale profounds with rustic highland melodies
Sonorous synthesisers with spontaneous reverie
The volcanic river comes dancing
Glee ascends onto the banks of a coast, bouncing
Robust arms of oaks vigors with fuel
Upland sterilises the ardour of bumps soaring gruel.

POEM: 36
Surrealism

Innocent heart descends the
utopic land
The glee of chocolates sips thou
sugary command
Unpleasant breeze accolades
the tic tac clock
Offspring twenties flirts and
mocks
Sipping thy sweetish divine
of realism
Grasping the horizon far of fanciful
surrealism
Honey of the stargaze pops thy
yearling
Smiles the sage eyes in sheer
Vaulting.

POEM: 37
Stigma

Look!! This lovely innocent girl
Dancing in rain
Who knows what is fading away from her life;
It might be her ambition!

The books were never opened.
Could have a reason out of fertilised education,
She was suffering from poverty
The little girl adjusted to that cruelty.

She was only fourteen
Who
Served the kitchen with her
cooking,
Unaware of the coming danger,
The innocent child turned into a
Kitchen manager
Though she was always
subordinate to her master.

The day came again
as she faced the brutal rain
couldn't reach home
for she was bound to be
sheltered in the master's room.

Shameful activities
She had never thought before,
She couldn't adjust to that cruelty
as she believed in the dignity
She lost her virginity
The master snatched her shyness
Lecturing child abuse should be

stopped and lots to modify.

Can one say what's more to modify?
Humanity is ashamed; it failed to
bring the lost glory,
What's more to specify?

But she is no more shy
Claiming justice for her
dignity, consoling words couldn't
make her glorified,
She has been molested everywhere in court, in public
and in media;
She struggled in between
the aristocratic manner in between
her battle with courage
occupying the baffled area.

She ultimately got the
justice, regaining her honour,
dignity, trust and confidence
Though she is unable to back
her virginity, but now she has
the proof of all consequences.

She has faced so bravely the
shame and humiliation
Statements after the statement, a lot of questions
Stupid asking for self-recognised
media and politicians.

An extreme provocation
She was against the offender,
revenge gave her satisfaction
So she could fight for all mothers
from generation to generation!

POEM: 38
Cursed Childhood

They are lovely
with the handful of winsome desire
ambitions won't be drained as if some satire.

They are lost in the crowds of hunger.
They wished to learn to play football
But time has snatched the rosy dreams
from their eyeball.

They wish to enter the school gate
Aah! Never have got a learned mate.

Their parents had kept lovely names.
Now those were lost in professional games
How could be so many chotus?
Making tea, polishing boots or begging in the queue.

No one seems to be their near
Can't anyone see those rolling tears?
They are also someone's dear,
Today nobody is with them to cheer
Compassion has turned into a queer
Still, they are sincere with their master
Destiny in the attire of sneer.

Though it's hard to bear that tear
They are used to render
They have lost their names and ambition in the wounds
of hunger.

They have no more wishes in this sphere
All chotus have given up their desires

In the struggle of a cruel life, they don't wish to be a teacher,
Even a doctor or an engineer
They are only the strugglers in the creation of the Super Master!

POEM: 39
Harmonic Song

Amidst the lovely silence
Drowsy eyes obey
it's reticence,
Darkness shelters in my palanquin,
In the lullabies of harmonic swing
In the lap of Mother Earth, very caring.

Tweeting good night to all of my lovelings
Meet you the other day, my dear siblings.
Till then, all of you do keep on smiling.

Maiden Moon is also offering
her affectionate greetings
Showering her love with peaceful blessing.

Peaceful rays of morning feeling of togetherness
with devotional praying,
Colours of the rainbow with the bond of trust and faith
The fragrance of brotherhood comes with lovely rose
buckets.

The birds are chirping the
harmonical song of kindness,
Wisdom blooms with merry of forgiveness.

The rocks and sand and non-living
take a bath in the waters of the ocean,
Giving equal nourishment
to all the siblings of His divine creation.

The harmonical song is blossoming
into a devotional flower,
Butterflies are gathering for the wisest nectar;

The river flows like a shy teenage girl
Flooding chaos from the icy glacier
Leaving all screams planting,
friendship beside streams
Prospering harmony into
a wonderful dreams
A smile of simplicity runs like a squirrel
Harmonical song remains
eternal.

POEM: 40
Peace, Omnipresent

When magical art
Showers of pleasant
rain
Come!!!
Nourish all pain.
Smile the azurine
grace
Wiping the dark clouds
from face.

Sorrows turn monk
preaching peace
Singing harmony with
shooting breeze
Compasionate touch of
affection in calmness
Kindness spreads everywhere
in silence.

Sublime attire of
nature
Motherly smelling
allover
Taking blessings from
rainwater
Rejoicing the very own
evergreen shelter
Trees leaning over on
one another
Rejecting the rotten leaves
over stagnant water
Buds are waiting to become

flower
Enjoying the silence
leaves are drinking water.

The serene track of
peace
Singing the harmonic song of wisdom
Smiles the wise feeling of detachment full of freedom.

Rejecting the old decorum
in rain
Flooding all pride and grievances
in lane
Relaxing in silence without any
complain
Peace smiles to nourish
again and again.

POEM: 41
To my Sister

Shine of sun
Song of my heart
You got the sweetest smile, O'Sister
The decor of my vase.

Colours of rainbow
The joy in my heart
You are my chocolate, Cadbury
Sweetest of the desserts.

You are my pride
Together we laughed and cried
Ocean of love and care
Nobody is as beautiful as my loving Sister.

Together we are friends forever.
I am the wings, and you are my feather
How do I fly alone?
A river without water!!
I feel so blessed to have you, oh dear Sister.

Always keep smiling
Remember, I do breathe within
The decor of every season
May it be a summer or an adorable spring.

POEM: 42
Sublime

I have seen the birds flying high
The wings bear numerous colour
Accept it, so love can prosper.

The radiance knocks the panes
Attending the scorching
temperature with high luminance
Fathom the glory of the brightness
An encounter to shine upto the
heights of merriness.

The palanquin of the balcony
Defeating the agony
Smiles in green
For the peaceful, serene
Pleasing is the climbers
Inspiring life's failures to achievers.

Comes the rain with so much thunder
Get wet and bear that revolver
Encourage life, and it's a circle to prosper.

I have seen the empty sparrow nest
Heard the giggle and zest
Amusing spirit of the tiny, pretty
sparrow
Accept it as life's yarrow.

Even failed to hold the sand in their hand
Still do borrow
It also bears the message
Do cultivate love rather damage.

9 798888 697771